4.Panzer-Division
on the Eastern Front (2) 1944

Text by Robert Michulec
Edited by Tom Cockle
Color plates by Arkadiusz Wróbel

CONCORD
PUBLICATIONS COMPANY

We welcome authors who can help
expand our range of books. If you
would like to submit material,
please feel free to contact us.

We are always on the look-out for new,
unpublished photos for this series.
If you have photos or slides or
information you feel may be useful to
future volumes, please send them to us
for possible future publication.
Full photo credits will be given upon
publication.

ISBN 962-361-649-X
printed in Hong Kong

The year 1944 started out ceremoniously. On January 31, 1944, the commander of the Division, Gen.Lt. Dietrich von Saucken was awarded the Swords to his Knight's Cross, the only such decoration to be won by any member of 4.Panzer-Division. The award was presented to him for his long service and leadership during the Division's successful operations in the summer and early autumn of 1943. In the latter months of 1943, the Division had not seen any significant action and very few decorations were awarded. During that time, the Division had been very weak, lacking replacements in men and equipment, including armored vehicles and transports.

The sector of the front controlled by 4.Panzer-Division was quiet, and the Division saw only limited offensive action late in 1943 and early 1944. The situation changed in early February, when they were incorporated into the Kampfgruppe created for the relief of Kovel, where the German garrison had been encircled by the Soviet Army. Almost at once, an attack to free the city was made from the west. It was led by XXXXII Armee Korps, commanded by Gen. Mattenklott, formed from 131.Infanterie-Division, 7.Hungarian Infanterie-Division and supported by 5.SS-Panzer-Division 'Wiking' and a few smaller units. The Kampfgruppe formed up on the line of the Bug River near the city of Dorohusk, which was connected to Kovel by a direct rail link. The attack proceeded along this line straight towards Kovel on March 19. Within the first three days, the Korps had advanced halfway to Kovel when the Soviets launched a counterattack to stop them. On March 26, Gen. Hossbach's LVI Panzer Korps, with 4. and 5.Panzer-Divisions and 28.Jäger-Division, came into action. 4.Panzer-Division, reinforced with Panzerkampfgruppe Muhlenkamp (SS-Obersturmbannführer Muhlenkamp, the commander of SS-Pz.Rgt.5), attacked from the north-west, finally breaking through the Soviet lines and entering Kovel on April 5, 1944.

After the success at Kovel, the Division spent the next 2 1/2 months in the relatively quiet rear area. During this time, they were involved in small scale actions, mainly against partisan groups. An increase in activity began to take place in early June 1944, when German Army intelligence first saw signs of Soviet preparations for an impending large scale offensive. Within two weeks, 4.Panzer-Division received new men and equipment including their second Panzer battalion, which had been training in Germany with their new 'Panther' tanks since the fall of 1943.

The new 1.Abteilung was equipped mostly with the Pz.Kpfw.V 'Panther' Ausf.A including a few early Ausf.G. New supplies of Pz.Kpfw.IV arrived as well, bringing the number of tanks in the Division up to 130. Pz.Jg.Abt.49 received several new Marder II self-propelled anti-tank guns and a few new Jagdpanzer IV. Pz.Aufkl.Abt.4 was re-equipped with Pz.Kpfw.II Ausf.L 'Luchs', a few light Sd.Kfz.222 and heavy eight wheeled Sd.Kfz.232 armored cars. Pz.Gren.Rgt.12 and 33 received a small number of Sd.Kfz.250 and Sd.Kfz.251 half-tracked personnel carriers, but not enough to equip even the first battalion of either.

A few days after the Soviet Army launched Operation 'Bagration', on June 22, 1944, 4.Panzer-Division was put on alert and was transported by train into the center of the typhoon which now raged across Belorussia. The German front was collapsing all around forcing individual divisions to fend for themselves as they retreated under constant pressure from the Russian onslaught. As the Germans slowly gave ground, pitch battles were fought for control of roads and bridges against the Soviet spearheads. Lack of transport and logistic support forced the German Army to conduct a series of fighting withdrawals, often unable to recover damaged vehicles from the battlefield which were quickly occupied by the Soviets. The number of Soviet prisoners taken was very small while losses were very high. A report on July 6, 1944 claimed the Division had killed 227 enemy soldiers, but no claims were made of prisoners taken. On the same day, 4.Panzer-Division destroyed 11 enemy tanks and 3 SPG's.

During the second half of July, as fuel and ammunition supplies became more critical, the Division was reinforced with 17 StuG.III of Stug.Abt.904 and 12 Tiger I Ausf.E of s.Pz.Abt.507. The addition of these vehicles gave the Division greatly needed support because of the serious depletion of the Division's own resources after several days of heavy fighting. On the evening of July 8, only 13 Pz.Kpfw.IV and 25 'Panther' tanks remained operational. All of the Division's armored vehicles had been thrown into the battle for Narew on July 17, 1944, when 4.Panzer-Division was sent to support 129.Infanterie-Division. With great determination, the German forces held back the attacks of the Red Army, which were uncoordinated and lacked air support. During two days of fighting on July 20 and July 21, 4.Panzer-Division counted 405 Soviet soldiers killed and only 25 wounded. Several guns were also captured. Losses to the Division by comparison were small and new replacements of armored vehicles had been received. On July 21, the combat strength of 4.Panzer-Division was:

Type of AFV	Ready for action	Repair within a few day	Repair within 3 weeks
Pz.Kpfw.V	13	27	27
Pz.Kpfw.IV	21	40	23
Panzerjäger	6	9	1
Jagdpanzer IV	-	4	16
StuG.III	8	16	1
Pz.Kpfw.VI	16	?	?
Pz.Bef.Wg.	6	-	-

After 2 weeks of heavy fighting, 8 StuG.III's, 12 Panthers and 3 Jagdpanzer IV's had been destroyed or damaged along with several other vehicles. By July 27, the combat strength was reported as follows:

Type of AFV	Ready for action	Repair within a few days	Repair within 3 weeks
Pz.Kpfw.V	32	27	9
Pz.Kpfw.IV	29	40	6
Panzerjäger	9	9	1
Jagdpanzer IV	5	1	14
Pz.Kpfw.VI	3	7	12
Pz.Bef.Wg.	6	-	-

At the end of July, 4.Panzer-Division started moving into the Warsaw area where they clashed with the Soviet 2nd Tank Army. The Division was divided into two battlegroups. Kampfgruppe Christern was composed of Pz.Rgt.35, Pz.Gren.Rgt.12, Pz.Aufkl.Abt.4, Pz.Pi.Btl.79, 3. and 4./Pz.Jg.Abt.79, H.FlaK.Abt.290 and fragments of Pz.Nach.Abt.79. Kampfgruppe von Gaudecker was composed of Pz.Gren.Rgt.33, Schützen-Rgt.1071 (an independent infantry regiment incorporated into the Division), I. and III./Pz.Art.Rgt.103, II./Pz.Art.Rgt.103, s.Pz.Abt.507, 1./Pz.Bau.Btl.159 and 1., 2., and part of 4./Pz.Jg.Abt.49. On August 1, the combat strength of the Division was as follows:

Type of AFV	Ready for action	Repair within a few days	Repair within 3 weeks
Pz.Kpfw.V	19	23	25
Pz.Kpfw.IV	28	18	17
Panzerjäger	12	2	2
Jagdpanzer IV	10	2	6
Pz.Kpfw.VI	29	15	-
Pz.Bef.Wg.	4	-	-

In total, there were 98 combat vehicles available for action, only 69 of which belonged to the Division.

During the first encounters with the enemy on August 2 and 3, 4.Panzer-Division claimed only 11 Soviet tanks destroyed. This number grew dramatically on August 4 to 53 and, altogether, during 8 days of devastating battle, a total of 108 tanks, 2 SPG's, 20 guns and 45 anti-tank guns. 544 Red Army soldiers had been killed and 52 captured. German losses were limited but the strength of the combat units was down to 2,325 men. On August 11, what was left of the men and equipment of the Division was transported to the Kurland Peninsula.

Again, the first clashes with the Soviet Army south-west of Riga were successful for 4.Panzer-Division. Within a few days, the Division claimed up to 1,000 Russian soldiers killed and about 200 captured. Also, there were about 200 guns and 100 tanks and SPG's destroyed or captured. The next two months were to be less active. On October 10, the Division had 819 combat troops in Pz.Gren.Rgt.12 and 33 and Pz.Aufkl.Abt.4, I./Pz.Gren.Rgt.33 had 231 men while I./Pz.Gren.Rgt.12 had only 115 men. They were closer to company rather than battalion strength.

The Division suffered further casualties between October 14 and November 3, in the defensive battles for the harbor at Libau. 4.Panzer-Division could only put into action 21 Pz.Kpfw.V 'Panther', 5 Pz.Kpfw.IV and 2 Jagdpanzer IV on October 17. With this small force, the Division counterattacked Soviet armored units in the area of the harbor and inflicted heavy losses on them. At the height of the battle, from October 27 to 29, 4.Panzer-Division claimed 57 tanks and SPG's destroyed, 23 of them on October 27 alone, when Kampfgruppe Christern and Kampfgruppe Hoffmann turned back 14 separate Soviet attacks. On this day the Division also claimed 25 guns destroyed and 200 enemy soldiers killed. In one duel, Lt. Kurze and the crew of his Pz.Kpfw.IV is credited with knocking out two T-34 tanks and one IS-2. Losses to the Division were 95 killed and 485 wounded. Despite these losses, on October 30, 4.Panzer-Division repulsed two strong Soviet attacks, destroying another 15 tanks and SPG's and 9 guns.

During the following weeks in Kurland, 4.Panzer-Division experienced periods of inactivity mixed with periods of heavy action, most of which occurred in late November and early December. There was a further lull in the action in early December, but in the last week of the month, from December 27 to 30, the Division was once more called upon to counterattack a Soviet breakthrough in the Skrunda-Saldus area. Pz.Gren.Rgt.12 was disbanded at this time because of its weakened condition and its remaining men absorbed into the other units. 4.Panzer-Division remained in the front lines until January 8, 1945, when they received orders to pull out of the line for transport to Danzig. In their final battle in Kurland, they added a further 67 tanks and SPG's destroyed or captured and 100 guns to the count.

In the middle of January, 1945, the remnants of 4.Panzer-Division made their way to Danzig. Their successes in Kurland had not been without cost. They had arrived as a weak, understrength unit and were now leaving having been further reduced to a Division in name only. Thus ends the story of 4.Panzer-Division in the Soviet Union which began 3 1/2 years earlier.

All photographs reproduced in this two volume story of 4.Panzer-Division are taken from albums prepared by G. Schlesener, which were found a few years ago in the Gdynia area. I was able to use them to create this book thanks to Mrs. M. Sulej and would like to express my gratitude for her co-operation and help.

After a long period of defensive operations, on December 20, 1943, 4.Panzer-Division took part in a limited offensive operation in the area west of Kiev, code named 'Nikolaus'. At this time, the total strength of the Panzerwaffe on the Eastern Front amounted to 2,280 tanks of which, only 915 were operational. This photo shows one of the few Sd.Kfz.251/7 Ausf.D engineering half-tracks from Pz.Pi.Btl.79. It appears to be a new vehicle as it is still painted in its factory dark sand finish.

This was the new emblem of 4.Panzer-Division introduced in early 1944 after the Divisional commander, Gen.Lt. von Saucken, was awarded the Swords to his Knight's Cross. The emblem was composed of the Divisional emblem first used in France in 1940, a man-rune within a circle, and crossed swords, both painted in yellow on a black shield background. The earlier emblem had seen limited use during 4.Panzer-Division's service in the Soviet Union and had been replaced with an arrowhead emblem in 1943. This emblem has been freshly painted on the mudguard of a Horch medium cross country car.

The same vehicle photographed shortly after, passing through one of the numerous Russian villages encountered by 4.Panzer-Division during its attack from the town of Osaritschi on the lower Dniepr River, in the sector of 9.Armee. The weather conditions in the last two weeks of December were excellent with clear skies and temperatures around -2ºC. The tubes being carried on the side of the vehicle appear to be stovepipes.

A Pz.Kpfw.V 'Panther' Ausf.A from one of the other Panzer-Divisions which fought along with 4.Panzer-Division during 'Nikolaus'. During this period, the Division's 'Panther' Abteilung was not available for combat. III./Pz.Rgt.15 was renamed I./Pz.Rgt.35 and converted to a 'Panther' Abteilung on September 24, 1943 and was still being trained in Germany. On December 20, 1943, the only vehicles the Division had at its disposal capable of dealing with Soviet tanks were 19 Pz.Kpfw.IV, including 5 received from 5.Panzer-Division, and 14 Panzerjäger.

An Sd.Kfz.7/2 armed with the 3.7cm FlaK36 anti-aircraft gun of Flak.Art.Abt.71 traveling through a Soviet village in the winter of 1943/44. The vehicle is fitted with an armor plate to protect the radiator but is lacking the armored cab. It appears to be painted in its original dark gray paint.

The mild weather at the end of December turned the roads into a morass which made offensive operations extremely difficult to carry out. Here we see a Pz.Kpfw.II Ausf.L 'Luchs' preparing to tow a Horch cross country car that has bogged down on a muddy village road. Behind this can be seen an Sd.Kfz.251/1 Ausf.D and an Sd.Kfz.10, also struggling with the poor conditions. The Sd.Kfz.251 appears to have received a new coat of white winter camouflage paint while the other vehicles still appear to be painted in their dark sand base color. The new Divisional emblem can be seen on the mudguard of the Horch.

A pair of Pz.Kpfw.V 'Panther' Ausf.A tanks, probably from SS-Panzer-Grenadier-Division 'Wiking', renamed 5.SS-Panzer-Division 'Wiking' in February 1944, which fought together with 4.Panzer-Division throughout the early months of that year. The officer running across in front of the Panther is wearing the SS fur lined anorak that was issued to SS troops during the previous winter.

A Pz.Kpfw.V 'Panther' Ausf.A passes by a Ford truck during Operation 'Nikolaus'. 4.Panzer-Division was involved in this operation with units of XXXXI.Pz.K. including 12.Panzer-Division, but on December 27, was pulled out of the front line to rest and refit. During the relief of Kovel a few months later, 4.Panzer-Division would fight alongside 5.Panzer-Division and 5.SS-Panzer-Division 'Wiking' under the command of LVI.Pz.K.

The battle against the environment was not restricted to daytime operations and, despite their predicament, these two Pz.Kpfw.II Ausf.L 'Luchs' crewmen can still manage to smile for the camera. Although it had only thin armor protection, the 'Luchs' was well liked for its speed and mobility. The method of attaching the spare idler wheel sections to the front of the hull is well illustrated in this photo. This vehicle is finished with a camouflage pattern of green or brown over the dark sand base and has a two digit tactical number painted in red on the turret.

An Sd.Kfz.165 'Hummel' heavy self-propelled howitzer armed with the 15cm sFH18 of Pz.Art.Rgt.103 towing a truck through a muddy field. This is an early production series vehicle with the raised compartment for the driver only. Later vehicles had a full width, simplified superstructure. It has a coat of white winter camouflage paint over its dark sand base and has the Divisional emblem painted on the side of the fighting compartment and a large letter 'G', indicating the seventh gun in the battery, probably painted in red.

A Pz.Kpfw.V 'Panther' Ausf.A of II./SS-Pz.Rgt.5 in the spring of 1944. It has been painted with a coat of white winter camouflage paint with the tactical number '835', probably painted in black. In September 1943, III./Pz.Rgt.15 was renamed I./Pz.Rgt.35 and sent to Germany to equip and train with the 'Panther'. So for a period of time, two I.Bataillon existed. The original I.Bataillon was on the front lines and on January 7 had 35 Pz.Kpfw.IV available. It was renamed II.Bataillon on January 8 and by January 21, the available number of tanks had dwindled to 2. There was a short period of time in March that it had no serviceable tanks at all!

An Sd.Kfz.10 leads a motorcycle combination down a flooded road in a Russian village. During the running battles of the winter of 1943/44, the lack of German success was rather a consequence of the conditions of the terrain and limited power of the German units than Soviet tactical skills.

Another view along the same road. This 'Panther' Ausf.A does not have a tactical number painted on the side of the turret but has, what appears to be, a shipping stencil on the gun cleaning rod tube and a national cross on the front hull side. The Zimmerit coating is quite clear in this photo.

A 'Panther' Ausf.A from 'Wiking' makes its way through a Russian village in the spring of 1944. Part of the tactical number, a white '4', can be seen on the rear turret hatch along with a national cross in the center of the rear plate between the exhaust pipes. The man standing on the engine deck on the right is also wearing the SS fur lined anorak. For the attack to open the Soviet encirclement of Kovel, SS-Pz.Rgt.5 was seconded to 4.Panzer-Division.

4.Panzer-Division took part in recapturing the city of Kovel which had been surrounded by the Soviet Army in mid-March, 1944. LVI Panzer-Korps, consisting of 4.Panzer-Division and 5.Panzer-Division, were deployed from the Brest-Litowsk area, arriving west of Kovel on April 3. The next day, the attack began, spearheaded by 4.Panzer-Division with the support of 131.Infanterie-Division and SS-Pz.Rgt.5, their northern flank protected by 5.Panzer-Division. The assault continued on April 5, when 4.Panzer-Division broke through the Soviet lines and established a permanent linkup with the defenders in Fortress Kovel.

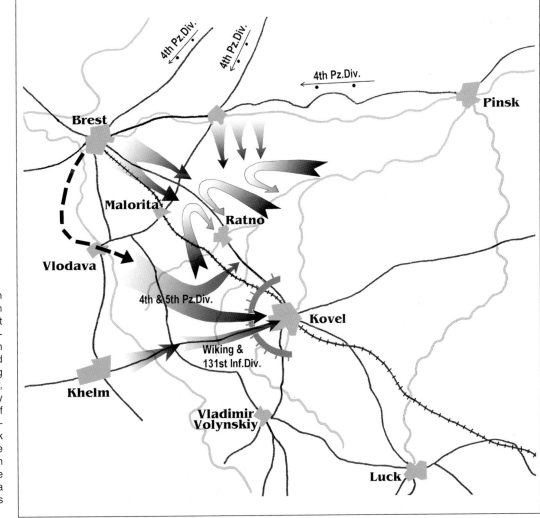

This 'Panther' is a very early Ausf.A built on the hull of an Ausf.D, which has probably lost its track to a mine. It is finished with a coat of white winter camouflage paint over the dark sand base. A patch of the base color has been left open on the turret for the tactical number '713' painted in either white or yellow. On April 4, 1944, the attack on Kovel began and a successful breakthrough the next day allowed some 2,000 German casualties to be evacuated out the corridor. The battle continued until Kovel was completely freed on April 24.

A Pz.Kpfw.II Ausf.L 'Luchs' of Pz.Aufkl.Abt.4 near Kovel. There were only 100 vehicles of this type built between September 1943 and January 1944 and 4.Panzer-Division was one of two Panzer Divisions to be fully equipped with them. The hulls and turret were similar to normal Pz.Kpfw.III design but the interleaved roadwheels owed their design to the 'Panther' and 'Tiger'.

Barely visible in the center of the photo is a British made Valentine tank that was abandoned by the Soviets during their retreat from outskirts of Kovel. 4.Panzer-Division knocked out 7 tanks repelling a Russian attack on April 10 in the Dubowa area north of the city. An abandoned T-34 was found by men of I./Pz.Gren.Rgt.33 and II./Pz.Gren.Rgt.12 in the area of the village of Moszezona, northwest of Kovel, to be in running condition and it was incorporated into the Divisional arsenal.

The front of an old Krupp Protz light truck is visible in this photograph taken on the outskirts of Kovel. In the background can be seen three 8.8cm FlaK36/37 anti-aircraft guns with white winter camouflage paint. At this stage of the war, there were very few of these trucks still in service with the Wehrmacht.

An Sd.Kfz.251 command half-track of either Pz.Gren.Rgt.12 or Pz.Gren.Rgt.33. The command flag on the left mudguard is black with a green horizontal stripe, the Panzer-Grenadiere branch of service color. Each Panzer-Division had two regiments of motorized infantry called Panzer-Grenadiere. Usually, only one battalion in each regiment was equipped with half-tracks and it was utilized in the assault. This vehicle appears to be finished in its factory dark sand paint.

The other battalions were equipped with trucks and were employed as normal infantry during attacks. The soldiers would ride on the tanks on the approach to the battlefield, whereupon, they would dismount and walk behind the tanks. Here, we see a troop of about twenty men preparing to attack near Kovel climbing aboard their transport into battle, a Pz.Kpfw.IV Ausf.G that is equipped with a full set of side skirts. It is also fitted with smoke grenade dischargers which can be seen just over the top of the turret skirt. On April 10, 4.Panzer-Division had only 19 of these vehicles left out of 30 available at the beginning of the month.

One of the supply trucks loaded with wicker ammunition cases has upset on one of the poor roads spilling its load. During wet spring and fall seasons, the logistic link for the Panzer-Divisions was stretched to the limit. Success on the battlefield could only be expanded upon with an adequate supply of fuel and ammunition over roads that were often inadequate and sometimes partly controlled by Partisans. In the background can be seen one of Pz.Aufkl.Abt.4's Pz.Kpfw.II Ausf.L 'Luchs'.

Several half-tracks from Pz.Gren.Rgt.12 or Pz.Gren.Rgt.33 crossing a field in the area of Kovel. On the right is an older model Sd.Kfz.251/3 Ausf.C radio vehicle of the battalion or company staff. On the left is an Sd.Kfz.10 and in the background is an Sd.Kfz.251/9 Ausf.D, armed with a 7.5cm KwK37 (L/24) howitzer. Two of the vehicles appear to have fairly new coats of white winter camouflage paint.

An Sd.Kfz.2 kleines Kettenkraftrad, or Kettenkrad for short, bogged down and abandoned on a muddy road in the area of Kovel in the spring of 1944.

A Pz.Kpfw.II Ausf.L 'Luchs' command tank of Pz.Aufkl.Abt.4, characterized by the star antenna. It is one of the newer vehicles received and lacks the smoke dischargers on the turret and the spaced front armor plate that identified the earlier ones. Their main role was that of reconnaissance which was limited during the battles around Kovel. On April 18, I./Pz.Rgt.35, supported by 3./Pz.Pi.Btl.79, repelled an attack in the area of Rudniki that cost the Soviets 7 of the 8 tanks they started out with. In battles like this, the 'Luchs' was of little use.

Another view of the same 'Luchs'. Note the splinter pattern Zeltbahn shelter quarter rolled up behind the Bosch headlight and the dust cover on the gun, perhaps indicating the photo was taken during a lull in the fighting around Kovel.

In this photo, taken somewhat later, the hinged front mudguard on the left side has been removed and has been placed on top of the main mudguard behind the Bosch headlight.

13

The first 'Panthers' appear on 4.Panzer-Division's strength report for April 17, 1944, while the battle for Kovel was still being fought . As I./Pz.Rgt.35 was equipped with Pz.Kpfw.IV at this time, these were probably vehicles from SS-Pz.Rgt.5 that were incorporated into the Division for this offensive. This is a Pz.Bef.Wg.V 'Panther' Ausf.A which displays markings for II.Abt. staff and has a rough coat of white winter camouflage paint. The markings are probably either yellow or a very dirty white. The star antenna mount can be seen on the rear engine deck but the antenna is missing. Also note the pistol port plug in the upper left corner of the number '0' on the turret side which indicates this is an early Ausf.A.

A late Pz.Bef.Wg.III Ausf.J of I./Pz.Rgt.35 following a column of Pz.Kpfw.IV across a snow covered field in March 1944. The three antenna are quite visible and a star antenna is mounted on the center of the rear engine deck. It does not have any white winter camouflage paint and remains in its original dark sand color. The tactical numbers on the turret skirt are not very clear but they look to be 'I02'.

Three Sd.Kfz.251/7 Ausf.D Pionierpanzerwagen parked by a farmhouse near Kovel. They are all finished in their dark sand base and the two in front have canvas covers over the crew compartment for protection against the weather. A spare roadwheel is hanging from the front plate of the vehicle on the right.

An early M4A2 Sherman tank knocked out by 4.Panzer-Division during the battle for Kovno. An internal explosion has ripped the turret from the tank, flipping it upside down and back on top of the hull. The crew of an Sd.Kfz.250/1 'Neu' give the hulk a casual glance as they pass by.

Another M4A2 Sherman knocked out just up the road is inspected by the crew of the Sd.Kfz.250/1. A tactical number '14' has been painted in white on the side of the turret and an illegible marking has also been painted on the applique armor plate on the side of the tank. The Soviet Army received 2,007 of the 75mm armed Sherman from the United States under the Lend-Lease program during WWII.

Two more victims of the German assault on Kovno, these 76.2mm Field Gun Model 1942/ZiS-3 were abandoned by their crews. They were dual purpose guns also capable of firing an anti-tank round. Produced in large numbers, they saw service well into the 1970's. In the background there are three Ford 'Maultier' half-track trucks, all finished in dark sand and one has a dark color canvas cover. Also visible is an Sd.Kfz.251/1 Ausf.D that has a coat of white winter camouflage paint. Note the contrast between the muddy suspension and the vehicle color.

The familiar Sd.Kfz.251/6 Ausf.B command half-track of Gen.Lt. von Saucken on the left and an Sd.Kfz.251/7 Ausf.D Pionierpanzerwagen on the right followed by one of the Division's early Pz.Kpfw.II Ausf.L 'Luchs' and two transport trucks. The assault bridges normally carried by the Pionier half-track are missing and a couple of wooden planks are in their place. It didn't take long for wet, muddy conditions to compromise the winter camouflage of these vehicles.

Two shots of a command version of the Pz.Kpfw.II Ausf.L 'Luchs' identified by the star antenna. In the above photo, the vehicle has become bogged down in the mud and the crew are working to free it. Even though it had a relatively high ground clearance, we can see that it has sunk down enough that the tracks can no longer move it. This is one of the original shipment of these vehicles received in the autumn of 1943 and has the spaced front armor plate and the spare idler rack on the front of the hull. The armor plate on the front of the 'Luchs' was only 30mm making it susceptible to small caliber Soviet anti-tank guns. The additional armor plate increased the protection to the equivalent of 50-60mm of armor plate.

During the battle for Kovel, 4.Panzer-Division's anti-tank unit took part in the action and proved itself one of the most important factors in the success of the operation. Pz.Jg.Abt.49 was armed with Marder II self-propelled anti-tank guns in two companies and towed 7.5cm PaK40 anti-tank guns in the third company. On March 30, there were 16 Marder II and 6 PaK40 available and during the next nine days, 10 of the Marder II were destroyed or damaged. The vehicle visible in the background is a 'Hummel' ammunition carrier.

During the rest period in March and the battles during April, the Division was protected against Soviet air attacks and supported in ground attacks by H.FlaK.Abt.290 which utilized the Sd.Kfz.10/4, such as this one armed with the 2cm FlaK38. Here we see one of them plowing its way down a muddy village road somewhere near Kovel.

17

Piles of ammunition for the 15cm sFH18 line the road in front of a church. Several RSO/01 are visible, perhaps suggesting they are being used to transport the ammunition to the gun emplacements.

An Sd.Kfz.251/1 Ausf.C, prominently displaying the new Divisional emblem on its front plate and carrying a row of replacement track links, passes through a Russian village. It has a coat of white winter camouflage paint over the dark sand base. Visible in the background is a Horch Kfz.17 heavy wireless car with the telescoping antenna extended. It appears to have a camouflage pattern of dark sand lines over its dark gray base.

An Sd.Kfz.8 half-track artillery prime mover pushes a wave of liquid mud before it as it makes its way through a Russian village. The temperatures during April fluctuated between -3ºC and +3ºC and coupled with light snowfalls and clear skies, the sun transformed the ground to mud. This made movement on both sides very difficult which slowed down and finally stopped all offensive actions. Note the specially made engine cover fabricated from straw woven into a blanket.

A column of BMW R75 motorcycle combinations make their way out of a Russian village past an immobilized Sd.Kfz.7, which has lost its right track. The motorcycles are from 5.SS-Panzer-Division 'Wiking' and appear to be still in their dark sand paint. The soldier in the sidecar and the rider are wearing the SS fur lined anorak. The driver also wears the rubberized motorcyclist's coat over his. Notice the license plate is missing off the mudguard of the first machine.

Up to mid-June, 4.Panzer-Division was not involved in any extensive operations, however, they did take part in some smaller anti-partisan actions. The time was utilized to train the few replacements and repair equipment. New vehicles began to arrive after June 10, just before the launch of Operation 'Bagration', the major Soviet summer offensive in Belorussia, on June 22, 1944. In this photo we see an older model Sd.Kfz.250/3 radio half-track that has been painted with a camouflage pattern of green and brown over the dark sand base and has a canvas cover over the crew compartment. Behind it can be seen an RSO/01 towing a heavily loaded trailer.

One of the last photos of 4.Panzer-Division in Kovel taken as an Sd.Kfz.251/1 Ausf.D passes through the city gates on its way out. The losses suffered during two weeks of fighting around the city were not high and equipment was quickly replaced. However, the Division did not receive enough men and equipment to replace the losses through the previous eight months. During the month of May and the first half of June, the Division rested but little was done to bring it back to full combat readiness.

An older model Sd.Kfz.251/1 Ausf.C with a heavy camouflage pattern of green and brown over the dark sand base. It had the Divisional emblem painted on the front but it has been obscured, probably by a censor. It also displays the vehicle license number WH-1540197 and has a small Iron Cross emblem painted on the top left corner of the front plate, possibly indicating a crew member has been awarded this decoration or, perhaps, a Knight's Cross. There is a small number '3' beside it which may indicate the company to which the vehicle belonged.

Dark storm clouds gather over these dug in and heavily camouflaged Sd.Kfz.251 half-tracks. There are probably six hidden in this field. The one on the right is an older Ausf.C model which still retains some of its white winter camouflage paint, while the one on the left is a newer Ausf.D in a dark sand finish. In early June 1944, 4.Panzer-Division was placed under command of H.Gr.Nordukraine.

An Sd.Kfz.251/1 Ausf.D as viewed through the open rear doors of an earlier Ausf.C. It has a camouflage paint scheme of green or brown applied over the dark sand base and is towing a small trailer of Soviet origin. It is also armed with an MG34 in place of the MG42 usually carried by these later vehicles.

Gen.Lt. Dietrich von Saucken in his Sd.Kfz.251/6 Ausf.B approaches the guard gate to the Division's encampment situated in a pine forest in Russia. As usual, von Saucken traveled in his very old, personal half-track equipped with the old style frame antenna for the long range radio sets carried in this type of vehicle. It carries the command pennants on its left mudguard and a horseshoe for good luck fixed to the front plate.

The vehicle has a camouflage pattern of brown and green over the dark sand base. Of special interest is the sign post on the left at the entrance with a carved wooden sign topped with a carved wooden tank, strangely resembling a Sherman, and inscribed with 'Saucken-hausen', literally 'Saucken's house'. Below it, a small Divisional emblem has been painted on the post. This was the occasion of Gen.Lt. von Saucken's farewell speech to the Division as he had been promoted to the command of XXXIX.Pz.K.

Gen.Lt. von Saucken visited the camp during the last days of his command in late April 1944. Here he is passing a new Pz.Kpfw.IV Ausf.H of I./Pz.Rgt.35 carrying the tactical number '425' on the turret skirt armor, indicating it is from 4.Kompanie. It is finished in a three color camouflage paint scheme of brown and green over the dark sand base. Standing in front of the tank, one of the soldiers can be seen wearing either a 'Kholm Shield' or 'Crimea Shield' on his left sleeve. On May 25, the Division had 61 Pz.Kpfw.IV Ausf.H available. This number rose to 70 by May 31 with 68 ready for operational use.

The lance pennants are more visible in this photograph as the General's half-track passes another Pz.Kpfw.IV Ausf.H. The pennants are made of metal painted with the black over white over red stripes for a Panzer-Division commander. The smaller pennant is unusual and may be painted on a yellow or darker white rectangular plate.

The Divisional emblem has been painted on the front plate of this Pz.Kpfw.IV Ausf.H with yellow markings on a black shield which also includes an inscription 'I./Pz.Rgt.35', a Panzer rhombus symbol and a number indicating the company to which the vehicle belonged.

A closeup of Gen.Lt. von Saucken standing in the crew compartment of his command half-track. The camouflage paint scheme is quite visible here with brown showing up as the darker spots and green showing up lighter.

Three photos showing Gen.Lt. von Saucken's farewell speech to the assembled men of 4.Panzer-Division. Command was turned over to Oberst Clemens Betzel, the commander of Pz.Art.Rgt.103, who was promoted to Gen.Maj. on July 1, 1944. Note the different camouflage schemes on both the Pz.Kpfw.IV Ausf.H. The bottom photograph shows the method of attaching the skirt armor very well.

The crew of this Pz.Kpfw.IV Ausf.H load ammunition for the tank's 7.5cm KwK40 L/48 main armament. The emblem on the side skirt is outlined in yellow and shows up well here indicating this vehicle is from 2.Kompanie of I./Pz.Rgt.35. The standing bear emblem of Pz.Rgt.35 is also just barely visible on the front of the turret skirt. The Feldwebel standing on the ground has been awarded two silver Tank Destruction Badges for the personal destruction of a Soviet armored vehicle.

A 4.Panzer-Division Leutnant picking up an MP40 off the front of a VW type 166 Schwimmwagen which has the Divisional emblem painted on it.

General Heinrich Eberbach, former commander of Pz.Rgt.35, inspects members of I./Pz.Rgt.35 on June 9, 1944. At this time, Gen. Eberbach was Inspector der Panzertruppen but on July 6, he was posted to France to take over command of Panzergruppe West.

On June 22, 1944, the Soviets launched Operation 'Bagration' in the sector controlled by H.Gr.Mitte and the following day, 4.Panzer-Division was put on alert, quickly loaded onto trains and sent north from Kovel. Here we see an Sd.Kfz.6/2 half-track armed with the 3.7cm FlaK36 anti-aircraft gun with its ammunition trailer in tow, from H.FlaK.Art.Abt.290. Just visible to the right is the front of a Soviet built truck.

At the beginning of July, the Division occupied a new defensive line on the Morocz River and held a bridgehead near the town of Cimkavicy, west of the city of Sluck. Here, 4.Panzer-Division met the Soviet Army head on and after three days of fighting was forced to fall back to Kleck on the Lan River. This damaged Pz.Kpfw.IV Ausf.H occupies a static defensive position. A white standing bear emblem followed by a black tactical number '121' and the new Divisional emblem are painted on the turret side skirt. The tactical number is repeated on the back of the turret skirt.

An infantry squad climb aboard a Pz.Kpfw.IV Ausf.H fitted with the wide 'Ostketten' and covered with a heavy application of Zimmerit. In the middle of June, 4.Panzer-Division finally received its 'Panther' Abteilung. The original I./Pz.Rgt.35, equipped with Pz.Kpfw.IV, was renamed II./Pz.Rgt.35. However, changing the numbering of the tanks did not happen immediately and so the Pz.Kpfw.IV continued to use their tactical numbering system starting with the numbers 1-4.

This closeup of a Pz.Kpfw.IV shows the unusual pattern of the Zimmerit which is probably a field application. A faint camouflage paint scheme can be seen on the hull side skirts. Note how scratched the paint is on the side skirts caused by brushing against trees and bushes. The tank commander is wearing his M1943 uniform tunic instead of his black Panzer jacket.

Another squad of Panzer-Grenadiere aboard a Pz.Kpfw.IV entering a village in the area of Cimkavicy in early July, 1944. At this time 4.Panzer-Division had 63 'Panthers' in I.Abt. and 34 Pz.Kpfw.IV in II.Abt. About 35 tanks had been left behind with another Panzer-Division still in the H.Gr.Nordukraine sector. 73 'Panthers' and 5 Pz.Kpfw.IV from 5.SS-Panzer-Division 'Wiking' were placed under command of 4.Panzer-Division for the battles in the H.Gr.Mitte sector, making it the strongest division available to them at the time.

A Pz.Kpfw.IV Ausf.H traveling down a road in western Belorussia in early July. By this time the Pz.Kpfw.IV was an obsolete design but improvements in armament and armor protection since spring of 1942 made it a worthy opponent on the battlefield to all but the powerful new IS-2.

The Pz.Kpfw.IV used by 4.Panzer-Division in July displayed a different camouflage scheme and tactical numbering style than those used in their earlier battles in May. It is likely that these older vehicles were left with H.Gr.Nordukraine when 4.Panzer-Division moved north. The same Pz.Kpfw.IV Ausf.H is shown here with markings clearly showing the standing bear emblem in white, the tactical number '500' in yellow and the new Divisional emblem painted on the turret side skirt. This vehicle is the command tank of 5.Kompanie of II./Pz.Rgt.35 and is painted with a three color camouflage scheme of brown and green over the dark sand base. Additional track links placed on the front of the tank gave an extra measure of protection and this enterprising crew has utilized some damaged Panther track links as well as some Sherman tracks.

Another shot of the same tank showing the hastily applied camouflage paint on the side skirts. This style was common on many of the Pz.Kpfw.IV Ausf.H utilized by the Division at this time.

Two MG42 machine gun teams await a ride on the tanks. Note the unusual camouflage paint on the helmets probably using paint intended for use on the armored vehicles.

Another MG34 team climb aboard a Pz.Kpfw.IV Ausf.H that has also been equipped with the wider 'Ostkette'. The side skirt plates were fitted with an adjustable lower bracket that pushed the bottom out to provide the additional space required by these wider tracks. This tank has a heavy coat of field applied Zimmerit as well.

After July 5, the Division continued to retreat to the west, all the time battling the hard pressing Soviet forces. The Germans defended a wide front in the Baranovichi area and tried to stop the Soviets on the Wiedzma, Szczara and Myszanka Rivers without success. In these photos we see two Pz.Kpfw.IV of II./Pz.Rgt.35 passing through a village and entering a forest area. The tank closest to the camera is a late Pz.Kpfw.IV Ausf.G or early Ausf.H. Lack of APC's forced the Germans to transport infantry squads on the tanks to provide protection against anti-tank ambushes.

Two Pz.Kpfw.IV carrying infantry in western Belorussia around July 10, 1944. The lead vehicle is the same one seen in the previous photo and has been well protected with the addition of spare track links around the front of the hull and turret. It also has the words 'Stur Heil', the meaning of which is not clear, painted on the front of the turret skirt. Note how the side skirts are hanging on the vehicle in the background, which has been fitted with 'Ostketten', compared with the vehicle in the foreground which is fitted with standard tracks.

The same late Pz.Kpfw.IV Ausf.G or early Ausf.H seen in the previous photographs giving a good view of the damaged side skirts. The rear skirt is missing and the support angle has been bent back causing the skirts to almost touch the ground. This shot also shows the white standing bear emblem painted on the turret skirt along with the tactical number '532' painted in yellow.

A Pz.Kpfw.IV Ausf.H displaying the white standing bear emblem and the Divisional emblem painted on the turret side skirt. Unfortunately, the tactical number is too faint to make out. It is finished in the standard three color camouflage scheme of brown and green over the dark sand base. On July 14, a small force of 14 Pz.Kpfw.V and 2 Pz.Bef.Wg.V, supported by StuG.III assault guns and anti-tank guns fought a battle for a bridge in Chorowicze, capturing 1 Soviet self-propelled gun and 21 anti-tank guns.

A late Pz.Kpfw.IV Ausf.G or early Ausf.H and two Pz.Kpfw.IV Ausf.H of 4.Panzer-Division make their way across a field in July 1944. Although the vehicles are camouflage painted, the schemes are quite different. The one on the left has large spots over the dark sand base and the other has a finer pattern of lines. In both cases, the Regimental and Divisional emblems are quite visible.

Two Zündapp KS750 motorcycle combinations along with an old Horch 830 B1 light cross country car from one of the Panzer-Grenadier Regiments, pause in a field along with an Sd.Kfz.251/1 Ausf.D. Both riders are wearing the motorcyclist's rubberized coat. On July 17, part of Pz.Gren.Rgt.12 was incorporated into Kampfgruppe Narew, based on the 129.Inf.Div. commanded by Gen. Merker, and took part in the battle for the Narew bridgehead.

An Sd.Kfz.251/1 Ausf.C from Pz.Gren.Rgt.12, transports its troop of Panzer-Grenadiere through a grain field in Kurland during the summer of 1944. It has a camouflage paint scheme of light green spots over the dark sand base with the tactical number '232' painted in black with a white outline and the Divisional emblem on the side of the hull. The tactical number indicates this is the 2nd vehicle in the 3rd platoon of the 2nd company.

An Sd.Kfz.251/1 Ausf.D makes its way through a small village. The tactical marking to the right of the spare tracks links indicates this vehicle is from 7.Kp. of either Pz.Gren.Rgt.59 or 112 of 20.Panzer-Division. The Division suffered heavy losses and the remainder was incorporated into 4.Panzer-Division in the middle of July, 1944. The camouflage pattern is composed of large areas of green and brown on the dark sand base.

More half-tracks in the same village accompanied by Pz.Kpfw.IV Ausf.H tanks, some of which may be from 12.Panzer-Division. Note how different the camouflage pattern on the tank to the extreme right is compared to the other photographs. There appears to be an oversize Iron Cross on the front plate of the tank facing the camera and it may, in fact, be a German wooden grave marker. The Divisional emblem is visible on the front plate of the Sd.Kfz.251/1 Ausf.C on the left.

Ford ''Maultier'', 4.Panzer-Division, Belorussia, spring 1944
This Ford ''Maultier'' half-track truck is finished in dark sand paint and carries a camouflage paint pattern of brown spots on the green canvas cover over the cargo compartment.

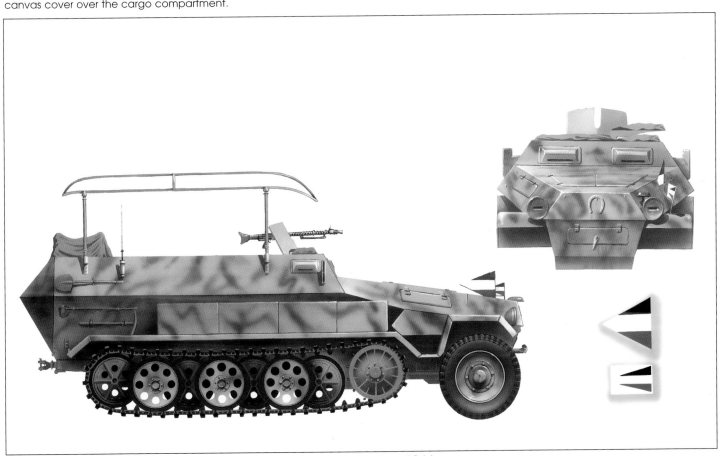

Sd.Kfz.251/6 Ausf.B, Stab 4.Panzer-Division, Eastern Front, spring 1944
This early Sd.Kfz.251/6 Ausf.B has been repainted with dark sand paint leaving only the frame antenna in the original dark gray finish. It has had a camouflage scheme of green and brown painted over and carries the command pennons for the commander of 4.Panzer-Division, Gen.Lt. Dietrich von Saucken.

Sd.Kfz.165 'Hummel', Pz.Art.Rgt.103, Kovel, spring 1944
This early production 'Hummel' has a white winter camouflage paint scheme that has been carefully applied over the dark sand base to leave the Divisional emblem exposed. The letter 'G' above indicates the seventh gun in the battery and is painted in red.

Pz.Bef.Wg.V 'Panther' Ausf.A, 5.SS-Panzer Division 'Wiking', Kovel, April 1944
II./SS-Pz.Rgt.5 was attached to 4.Panzer-Division for the battles in the Kovel area in April 1944. This is a II.Abt. staff vehicle which has been painted with a white winter camouflage paint and carries the tactical number '1102', most likely in yellow paint on the turret. The star antenna normally carried on the rear of the engine deck is missing.

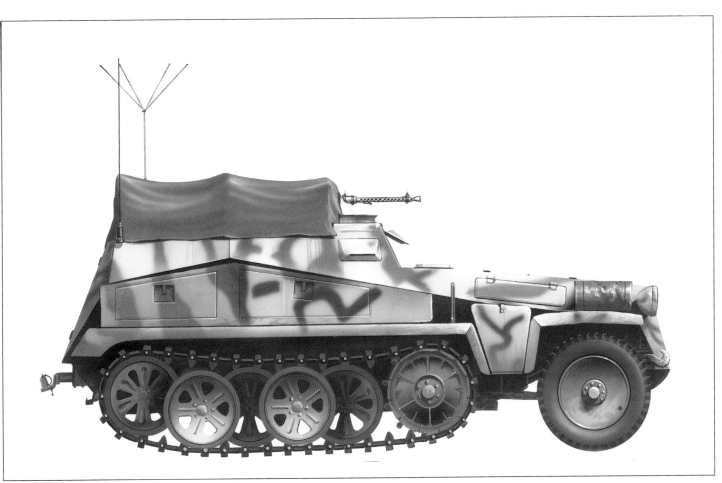

Sd.Kfz.250/3, Stab 4.Panzer-Division, Belorussia, June 1944
This early model Sd.Kfz.250/3 leichter Funkpanzerwagen carries a three color camouflage pattern of brown and green lines over the dark sand base. No other markings are evident. It is fitted with a 2 meter star antenna for the FuG 12 radio set and a canvas cover over the crew compartment.

Pz.Kpfw.IV Ausf.H, II./Pz.Rgt.35, Belorussia, July 1944
With the arrival of the 'Panther' Abteilung, I.Abt. was renamed II.Abt. and all the Pz.Kpfw.IV were renumbered. This Pz.Kpfw.IV Ausf.H, formerly of 1.Kompanie, was renumbered with a yellow '500' for a 5.Kompanie vehicle. The Regimental standing bear emblem is painted in white and the new Divisional emblem has been applied on the turret side skirt. It consisted of a black shield with the old Divisional emblem and other markings added in yellow. The vehicle carries a three color camouflage scheme typical for tanks of this unit at the time.

Sd.Kfz.6/2, H.FlaK.Art.Abt.290, Belorussia, July 1944
This vehicle carries a camouflage scheme of irregular green spots over the dark sand base. The 3.7cm FlaK36 anti-aircraft gun is still finished in its original dark gray paint.

BMW R75 Motorcycle Combination, Poland, July 1944
This BMW R75 motorcycle combination has a very unusual camouflage scheme of wide green lines with narrow dark brown lines painted over the dark sand base. The soldiers helmets have been painted in the same manner. Notable among the Division's motorcycles is the lack of standard license plates normally mounted on the front mudguard.

Pz.Kpfw.V 'Panther' Ausf.A, I./Pz.Rgt.35, Poland, July 1944

This Panther Ausf.A is painted with a three color camouflage scheme of green and brown lines and patches over the dark sand base. It has, what appears to be, several additional track links stowed along the side above the log. A white tactical number, '113', has been painted on the turret and a black number '8' appears on the front side skirt, the meaning of which is unknown. The plate that it is painted on, however, is possibly from another vehicle as it has notches in front indicating it is not in its original position.

Pz.Bef.Wg.V 'Panther' Ausf.G, I./Pz.Rgt.35, Poland, July 1944

This Panzerbefehlswagen 'Panther' Ausf.G is painted in a standard three color camouflage scheme of green and brown over the dark sand base and carries the standard antennae for the FuG 5, FuG 7 and FuG 8 radio sets. The tactical number, '182' painted in yellow on the side of the turret is unusual as the number '8' would normally be a lower number.

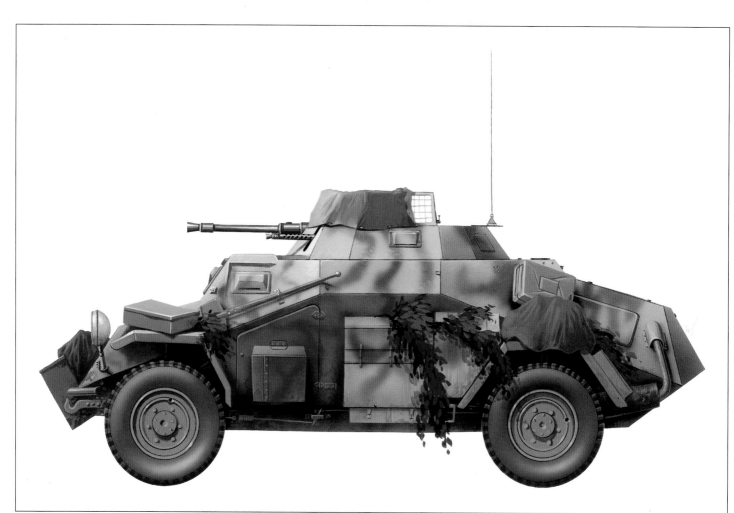

Sd.Kfz.222, Pz.Aufkl.Abt.4, Kurland, August 1944
This late model Sd.Kfz.222 has been painted in a three color camouflage scheme of green and brown lines over the dark sand base along with some cut foliage draped over the vehicle.

Sd.Kfz.251/1 Ausf.D, Pz.Gren.Rgt.12 or 33, Kurland, August 1944
An Sd.Kfz.251/1 Ausf.D of one the Panzer-Grenadier Regiments of 4.Panzer-Division with a camouflage scheme of green and brown wavy lines applied over the dark sand base. The tactical number '931', is painted in black with a white outline. The national cross, painted on the upper hull at the rear of the vehicle, is located in an unusual spot. It was usually painted lower, on the space between the last two storage bins.

Sd.Kfz.251/3 Ausf.D, Stab Pz.Gren.Rgt.33, Kurland, August 1944

The command half-track of Pz.Gren.Rgt.33, this vehicle is painted with a camouflage scheme of light green spots over the dark sand base. The tactical number '3301', is painted in black with a white outline along with the Divisional emblem and the tactical sign for a Panzer-Grenadier-Regiment headquarters painted in white below it. The command pennant for a Panzer-Grenadier-Regiment, black with a green stripe and carrying the Divisional emblem on it, is mounted on the left mudguard. The small Iron Cross emblem represents the Knight's Cross won by the Regimental commander.

Sd.Kfz.251/1 Ausf.C, Pz.Gren.Rgt.12, Kurland, summer 1944

This vehicle has been painted with a camouflage scheme of green spots over the dark sand base. The tactical number '232' is painted in black with a white outline and the Divisional emblem has been painted under the visor. The national cross is an older narrow style.

Pz.Kpfw.V 'Panther' Ausf.G, I./Pz.Rgt.35, Kurland, September 1944

This Panther Ausf.G has an interesting camouflage pattern of green lines and spots applied over the hull and turret. The gun barrel is darker, possibly indicating it is a replacement barrel. Spare track links have been attached to the turret in an unusual manner and the tactical number, a white '113' has been painted on them.

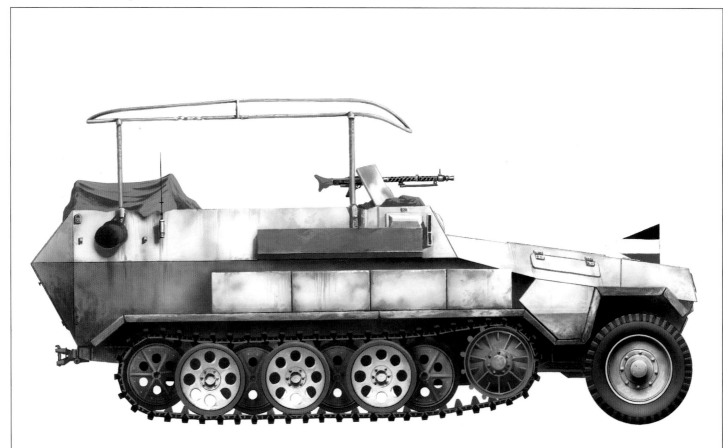

Sd.Kfz.251/6 Ausf.B, Stab 4.Panzer-Division, Kurland, December 1944

This Sd.Kfz.251/6 Ausf.B command half-track, now used by the new Divisional commander, Gen. Betzel, has been painted with a white winter camouflage scheme over the dark sand base and carries the Divisional command pennant on the left mudguard. A wooden box has been fitted to the right side for vehicle tools or equipment. This vehicle saw almost continuous service with 4.Panzer-Division on the Eastern Front.

A column of Pz.Kpfw.IV Ausf.H advancing down a dirt road. Its crew have added some additional protection, in the form of Sherman track links, to the front of the hull. The battle for the Narew bridgehead lasted from July 17 to July 20. At this time, 4.Panzer-Division held about 40km of the frontlines along with other, small supporting units from 129.Inf.Div., 4.Kav.Brig. and StuG.Brig.904. The next 20km was held by StuG.Abt.118, s.Pz.Abt.507 and three infantry regiments.

The same column a short distance further up the road, pass an Sd.Kfz.251/1 Ausf.D stopped at the side. On July 21, 4.Panzer-Division struck a wing of the Russian forces, inflicting heavy losses and disintegrating the Soviet lines. The next day, an attack by Kampfgruppe Christern in the area of Bielsk Podlaski resulted in a battle for Kleszcze. Here, troops of 5.SS-Panzer-Division 'Wiking' were encountered.

Almost a full company of Pz.Kpfw.IV Ausf.H from II./Pz.Rgt.35 make their way across a field in Poland, July 1944. A colorful blanket has been placed over some the crew's personal equipment on the right mudguard of the leading vehicle. On the evening of July 21, 4.Panzer-Division reported a strength of 6 Pz.Bef.Wg, 13 Pz.Kpfw.V, 21 Pz.Kpfw.IV, 8 StuG.III, 6 self-propelled guns and 16 Tiger I from s.Pz.Abt.507. The rest of the Division's vehicles were unserviceable.

The new commander of 4.Panzer-Division, Gen.Maj. Betzel, seated in his Horch Kfz.70 staff car during a visit to the front. He is wearing a personally tailored tunic made from the standard Wehrmacht splinter pattern camouflage material. Seated next to him, wearing the black Panzer uniform, is a young Leutnant of Pz.Rgt.35. The Horch carries an interesting variation of the Divisional emblem, painted on an elongated shield and featuring the tactical marking for 4.Panzer-Division that was normally used on maps and charts.

This Horch heavy cross country car has been heavily camouflaged with foliage to break up its shape. The passenger on the left appears to be wearing a helmet that has been painted with dark sand camouflage paint. During the battles in July against the Soviets, the Division claimed 86 tanks and self-propelled guns destroyed as well as 589 guns of different types. More fighting took place later in the month in the Warsaw area when, on July 29, a reconnaissance troop attacked a Russian artillery position and destroyed five 122mm howitzers.

Another photo of the Pz.Kpfw.IV Ausf.H with the tactical number '500' taken later shows some damage that has occurred during the battles of the previous weeks. One of the side skirts has been lost and the others are hanging in disarray. The crewman standing on the front of the tank appears to be wearing the arm and hatband of a wargame's umpire, though it is not clear why, given the situation, such games would be conducted.

A BMW R75 motorcycle combination that has a very unusual camouflage paint scheme of wide green lines with very dark brown, narrow lines over the dark sand base. The men riding the motorcycle and some of the men standing on the Pz.Kpfw.IV Ausf.H in the background have painted their helmets in the same pattern, also seen in previous photos. Note how most of the Division's motorcycles we have seen do not have license plates on the front mudguards.

A Pz.Kpfw.V 'Panther' Ausf.G of I./Pz.Rgt.35 moves slowly along a road in Poland. After the heavy fighting in the Narew area, the northern flank of H.Gr.Mitte was stabilized somewhat and 4.Panzer-Division was given a short rest period at the end of July. An order was received to transport the Division to the Warsaw area where strong Soviet forces appeared. H.FlaK.Abt.290, the first unit to arrive at Wyszkow, just north of Warsaw, was surprised by a Soviet attack on August 1 and lost all their ammunition transport.

Another Pz.Kpfw.V 'Panther' Ausf.G, following close behind, is passed by a battery of horse drawn artillery towing 7.5cm le IG18 infantry guns. The tactical number indicates this is the 1st tank of the 1st platoon of the 3rd company in I.Abt. Throughout the whole war, the Germans relied heavily on the use of horses.

Gen.Maj. Betzel looks out on the battlefield from his Sd.Kfz.251/6 command half-track in late July, 1944. The General inherited command of the Division, but it does not look like he inherited General von Saucken's command half-track. The camouflage pattern on the front is quite different from that of General von Saucken's early Sd.Kfz.251/6 Ausf.B.

An early production Pz.Kpfw.V 'Panther' Ausf.G with the tactical number '311' painted in white is finished in a camouflage scheme of light green and brown spots over the dark sand base. The main opponent of the 'Panther' in the summer of 1944 was the T-34/85, which was not as well armored and was armed with a less potent gun. Note the long pry bar still mounted on the brackets that previously supported the gun cleaning rod tube. This is not normally visible because it is hidden behind the tube.

Another 'Panther' Ausf.G on the same road with the tactical number '331' indicating it is the 1st tank in the 3rd platoon of the 3rd company. As the 'Panther' Abteilung had only arrived in June, there had been no time to paint the Divisional emblem on the turrets as had been done with Division's Pz.Kpfw. IV's. Both of these Panthers have the gun cleaning rod tube relocated to the rear of the engine deck.

Two 'Panther' Ausf.A following behind also have their gun cleaning rod tubes attached to the rear of the engine deck. Unfortunately, the late day lighting makes it difficult to make out the camouflage paint schemes on these vehicles. The fact the crews are riding outside the tanks would indicate they are not in any immediate danger from the Soviet Army.

More 'Panthers' of I./Pz.Rgt.35 make their way across a small pond of water in the road through a Polish village. The truck parked at the side of the road is a Soviet ZIS vehicle that has been captured by the Division and has been painted in standard German camouflage paint. Many captured vehicles were used by the Germans until they wore out and were abandoned for lack of spare parts. This truck has a Wehrmacht license plate indicating that it was incorporated into the German Army officially.

A 'Panther' commander posed in the classic style in his cupola. The Pz.Kpfw.V 'Panther' Ausf.A is coated with Zimmerit and has a camouflage pattern of brown or green over the dark sand base. The tactical number '212' has been painted on the side of the turret in white. It is carrying a large, wooden unditching beam on the side, supported on the side skirts. The 7.5cm KwK42 L/70 tank gun is supported on the raised travel lock but is not secured, leaving the gun free in case a sudden need arises. The roadwheels appear to be wet, perhaps having recently passed through the same pond as the tanks in the above photo.

This Pz.Kpfw.II Ausf.L 'Luchs' is one of the later production vehicles received by Pz.Aufkl.Abt.4. Note the amount of loose equipment stored on the vehicle and the additional storage box mounted on the rear of the mudguard by the Division workshop. The object sitting in front of it is a 3kg hollow-charge anti-tank mine.

An Sd.Kfz.250/3 crewman salutes as his vehicle passes by an Sd.Kfz.251 command half-track. Visible markings are the tactical number, probably '802', painted in white on the side, the license number WH-1448159, a small, unidentifiable marking in a dark square on the upper left side of the front plate and a barely identifiable Divisional emblem on the upper right.

This 'Panther' Ausf.A with tactical number '113' carries several additional track links supported by the long unditching log on the side of the hull. The gun cleaning rod tube normally fixed here has been moved to the rear of the engine deck. There is an unusual, black number '8' painted on the front side skirt. The notch in the front of the skirt plate identifies it as originally coming from farther along the side of this, or possibly another, vehicle. A three color camouflage paint scheme has been applied.

Command half-track of Pz.Gren.Rgt.33 with the Regimental commander, Oberst von Gaudecker, standing in front. This Sd.Kfz.251 Ausf.D has been field modified from its original form to serve as a radio command vehicle. There are two antenna bases on the right side and the crewman in the rear is wearing radio headphones, but there are no visible antenna. The tactical number '3301' is painted in black with a white outline and indicates this to be the command vehicle of Panzer-Grenadier-Regiment 33. The Regimental command flag is carried on the left mudguard and is black with a green stripe and has the Divisional emblem painted on it along with an Iron Cross emblem symbolizing the Knight's Cross won by Oberst von Gaudecker. On the right side of the driver's compartment, the Divisional emblem is repeated along with a faint tactical sign for a Panzer-Grenadier-Regiment below it.

Staff personnel view the battlefield from their command half-track through field glasses and a scissors periscope mounted behind the protective MG42 gun shield.

The same officers studying a map along with Oberst von Gaudecker. The Divisional emblem identifies this Sd.Kfz.251 to be the command half-track of Pz.Art.Rgt.103. A shipping stencil has been painted just below the driver's vision slit and a swastika has been painted on the right, an extremely rare marking for an armored vehicle.

A Panzer-Grenadiere climbs into his Sd.Kfz.251/1 Ausf.D half-track on a dirt lane in a Polish village. Even though the vehicle has rear doors, it was often easier to climb over the side because of the amount of equipment stowed in the interior. This vehicle has the tactical number '113' painted in black with a white outline on the rear along with the Divisional emblem and a narrow national cross. The '1's in the tactical number are unusual in that the white outline on the left side of the vertical bar extends up through the diagonal tail. Also visible just to the right of the bundle of straw is a small black Iron Cross outlined in white, symbolic of the Knight's Cross awarded to the Regimental commander.

Another photo of 'Panther' '113' heavily camouflaged with straw sitting in a field in Poland. Self preservation often provided the inspiration can in camouflage techniques, an art of war the Germans were masters of.

Two Pz.Bef.Wg.V 'Panther' Ausf.G follow a standard combat version past a grain field in the summer of 1944. The three antenna on each vehicle can be seen including the characteristic star antenna for the FuG8 radio set.

Three Pz.Kpfw.V 'Panther' Ausf.G passing through a small village. The partially visible tactical number on the last tank indicates it is from 2.Kompanie. The 'Panther' gave to 4.Panzer-Division crews, a battlefield superiority only compromised by lack of fuel and ammunition during this stage of the war. Since its debut in 1943, the 'Panther' had been continually upgraded and represented the peak of German tank design. On July 31, 1944, Pz.Rgt.35 reported strength was 28 Pz.Kpfw.IV and 19 Pz.Kpfw.V available for combat with 40 Pz.Kpfw.IV and 48 Pz.Kpfw.V in need of long and short term repairs. While the number of serviceable Pz.Kpfw.IV remained fairly constant since the beginning of July, the number of serviceable 'Panthers' was down by almost 50%.

A Pz.Kpfw.V 'Panther' Ausf.A fords a small stream past one of the Divisional half-tracks. No tactical number is evident but there is a small national cross on the front side of the hull. During the latter part of 1944, the 'Panther' formed the mailed fist of 4.Panzer-Division.

A Pz.Bef.Wg.V 'Panther' Ausf.G at rest in a grain field. The tank belonged to the staff troop of I./Pz.Rgt.35 and carries some unusual markings. The tactical number 'I82' is painted on the side of the turret in yellow. The 'I' represents I.Abt. but it is not clear what the '8' represents and may just be a non-standard system employed by the troop. The '2' indicates this is the 2nd vehicle of the staff troop. The vehicle is camouflaged with the standard three color scheme of green and brown over the dark sand base.

The driver of this Kfz.2 Kettenkrad has brought mail from home to one of the crew members of this Pz.Kpfw.V 'Panther' Ausf.A. Tow cables have been attached to the front tow hooks so that they can be quickly utilized if needed. On July 8 and 9, there were 4 Pz.Kpfw.IV and 10 'Panthers' out of service due to damage and breakdowns. The crew has removed the gun cleaning rod tube to the rear of the engine deck, typical for 'Panthers' of this unit. Note the small puppy on the glacis just above the MG ball mount.

An Sd.Kfz.9 half-track prime mover attempts to retrieve this Pz.Kpfw.V 'Panther' Ausf.A from the soft ground it has become bogged down in. The tactical number '334' is painted in yellow on the side of the turret. Originally, the tactical number of the different companies were painted in different colors but this practice was dropped in 1942-43 in favor of red, white or black numbers. 4.Panzer-Division used mostly yellow numbers. Note the Divisional emblem painted on the back of the half-track.

This wooden cab Ford 'Maultier' half-track makes its way over a road that has been built up by placing cut branches and trees over the soft ground similar to corduroy roads built through swampy areas. This is a new vehicle finished in overall dark sand and was probably one of those shipped to the Division with the 'Panthers' of I./Pz.Rgt.35.

A late model Sd.Kfz.222 from Pz.Aufkl.Abt.4 photographed somewhere in the Kurland pocket in late August 1944. The Division was transferred to this area from Warsaw and moved into the northern flank of the German defense on August 11. Two days later, on August 13, they were involved in battles in the area of Schagaren. At this time the Divisional strength was not great, with only 2,325 fighting men, but they had about 100 serviceable tanks which helped put up a strong defense where it was sorely needed.

A 'Hummel' self-propelled howitzer crossing a small wooden bridge across one of the dozens of small rivers and streams encountered by the retreating troops of 4.Panzer-Division in western Belorussia and eastern Poland. 'Hummels' had been employed in the Division's Pz.Art.Rgt.103 since the summer of 1943. Note the two color camouflage scheme of green spots over the dark sand base. The Divisional emblem can be seen on the front of the crew compartment. During 8 days of heavy fighting east of Warsaw from August 2 to 9, 4.Panzer-Division claimed 544 Soviet soldiers killed and 108 tanks, 2 SPG's, 20 field guns and 45 anti-tank guns destroyed.

Two 'Panthers' of I./Pz.Rgt.35 hidden in a forest somewhere between Moscheiken and Mitau, to the southwest of Riga. Under the command of Major Schultze, the Abteilung experienced several successful engagements with the Soviet forces opposed to it. During the first few days, the Division destroyed or captured up to 100 guns, 20 tanks and SPG's, killed over 500 enemy soldiers and captured 150 more.

Many of the battles against the Soviets in Kurland in 1944 were conducted by small battlegroups called Kampfgruppen. Kampfgruppe Christern was formed on Pz.Rgt.35 and included Pz.Aufkl.Abt.4 under Hptm. Moler. Here we see one of their vehicles, an Sd.Kfz.250/1, one of the older models that has been modified with the addition of storage compartments over the mudguards which gave it a similar appearance to the later 'Neu' version.

An Sd.Kfz.251/1 Ausf.D with the tactical number '931' painted in black with a white outline and the national cross displayed in an unusual location, high on the back of the crew compartment. It is finished in a camouflage scheme of green and brown irregular lines over the dark sand base. Like most other Divisions at the time, 4.Panzer-Division was short of soft-skinned vehicles for transport and supply and the situation with light armored vehicles was not much better. The real power of the Division was in Pz.Rgt.35, though large numbers of tanks were unserviceable and requiring repairs.

A German mechanic services the roadwheels of an Sd.Kfz.251 at night. 4.Panzer-Division suffered most of its losses due to mechanical breakdowns and not to enemy fire, which placed a great strain on the service battalion to keep the vehicles of the Division in running condition. Note how badly worn the rubber tire is on the outside rim of the wheel.

This Pz.Kpfw.V 'Panther' Ausf.A has suffered a breakdown and is being towed by another 'Panther' to the workshop for repairs. The turret has an oakleaf pattern of camouflage paint applied in green and brown while the hull appears to be in the dark sand base only. It was usually forbidden for tanks to tow each other but sometimes the situation dictated otherwise.

A 15cm sIG33 Ausf.H 'Grille' self-propelled howitzer, constructed on the chassis of the Pz.Kpfw.38(t), of Pz.Art.Abt.103 followed by an old Horch 830 B1 light cross country car. In the background, just in front of the 'Grille', an Sd.Kfz.251 can be seen.

A heavily camouflaged Pz.Bef.Wg.V 'Panther' Ausf.G waits in a field for the enemy to appear. The main Soviet anti-tank weapons were anti-tank rifles and 45 and 57mm light anti-tank guns which were ineffective against the 'Panther' and, in many cases, the Pz.Kpfw.IV. Most of the German tank losses were caused by minor damage rather than total destruction. The object across the back of the engine deck is two wooden ladders.

Some of the local civilian population look on with amusement at this Pz.Bef.Wg.III Ausf.M that has broken through a wooden bridge and fallen into a small stream. It has been fitted with the short barrel 5cm gun and early pattern 8 hole drive sprocket, with a spacer ring to accommodate the 40cm track, and carries the Divisional emblem painted on the turret side skirt. There were 3-4 of these vehicles available to the staff of Pz.Rgt.35 in August and September 1944. By this time, the Pz.Kpfw.III was still a reliable vehicle requiring minimal maintenance.

A battle hardened veteran, this Pz.Kpfw.IV Ausf.H has lost its side skirts and has been heavily camouflaged with foliage by its crew, typical for 4.Panzer-Division vehicles in Kurland. The tank crews proved to be well trained and determined soldiers during the early battles in Kurland, inflicting heavy casualties on the enemy with minor casualties of their own. On August 20, they destroyed 5 Russian tanks, including 2 IS-2, 50 guns, 4 tractors, 2 armored cars and killed or captured 135 Soviet soldiers.

Another photo of the Pz.Bef.Wg.V 'Panther' Ausf.G of the regimental staff crossing a grain field in August 1944 near the village of Levalaisi. On August 20, about the time this photo was taken, Kampfgruppe Christern won a major battle in the area of this village against a superior Soviet force. Over a period of 12 hours, the Germans claimed 12 tanks destroyed, including 9 IS-2, and about 5 guns. Of the 15 IS-2 committed to the battle, 7 were destroyed by the 'Panther' crews of I./Pz.Rgt.35. Note the different camouflage patterns carried on the turret and gun barrel and the hull. The Kurland landscape was dotted with many small forests and the addition of foliage as camouflage was common.

Two more shots of the Pz.Bef.Wg.V 'Panther' Ausf.G approaching the burning village. The 'Panthers' of I./Pz.Rgt.35, supported by Pz.Gren.Rgt.12, were involved in heavy fighting during the day and into the night of August 22. The enemy was overwhelmed and the Division claimed 16 Soviet tanks destroyed. II./Pz.Rgt.35 did not fare as well, losing their commander who was wounded during the attack.

This Sd.Kfz.251/1 Ausf.C, identifiable only by the small part of the engine deck exposed among the heavy camouflage, moves through a recently harvested grain field near a burning village in late August 1944. The last days of August were spent in battles in the area of Autz, where the commander of II./Pz.Gren.Rgt.12, Hptm. von Gaupp was wounded by an anti-personnel mine on August 24.

An Sd.Kfz.251/1 Ausf.C approaches the same burning village. These vehicles have been heavily camouflaged with foliage fixed to sides of the crew compartment to blend in with their surroundings. The attacks in the Autz area began on August 24. On the first day, the Division captured a forest near the village that had been occupied by strong Soviet forces, capturing or destroying 16 anti-tank guns, 13 field guns and 2 tanks.

This Sd.Kfz.251 is so heavily camouflaged with foliage that identification is impossible. There was only one battalion of APC's in each Pz.Gren.Rgt. of 4.Panzer-Division, which were in fact, closer to company strength. Based on the number of soldiers in each battalion, which was limited to about 200 men at this time, there should have been 15-20 Sd.Kfz.251/1 in each battalion.

General Betzel, commander of 4.Panzer-Division, receives a situation report from one of his officers during the battle. He is riding in his heavily camouflaged Sd.Kfz.251/6 Ausf.B command half-track. The first day of action resulted in destroying 22 tanks and SPG's, 34 guns and 9 other vehicles in addition to 105 Russian soldiers killed and 43 captured. It was for these battles in late August, that Gen. Betzel was awarded the Knight's Cross on September 7, 1944.

After the capture of the village, strongpoints were prepared at once in case of enemy counterattacks. Somewhere in the rear area, a command point would be set up to monitor and transmit radio signals. There are actually three Sd.Kfz.251's in this photo. The one in the foreground is an Sd.Kfz.251/1 Ausf.D while the one behind it is an Sd.Kfz.251/3, identifiable by the star antenna for the FuG 8 radio and the FuG Spr.f antenna in front. Another antenna is faintly visible beyond, indicating the presence of another vehicle.

A Pz.Kpfw.V 'Panther' Ausf.A struggles up a steep hill. It is easy to see in this photo how vulnerable the tank would be to enemy gunfire as it crested the hill. The tanks of I./Pz.Rgt.35 claimed 25 Soviet tanks knocked out in 3 days between August 25 and August 27, 1944. In addition, there was 1 SPG, 15 guns and 3 soft-skinned vehicles destroyed. I./Pz.Rgt.35 used only two models of 'Panther', the Ausf.A and Ausf.G.

A late model Pz.Kpfw.IV Ausf.G with the later style commander's cupola. The tactical number '621' is painted in a white outline style on the turret skirt. The tank is in relatively good condition for this late stage of the war.

II./Pz.Rgt.35 played a minor role in the later battles in Kurland. This was due to the high rate of attrition as a result of breakdowns among the Pz.Kpfw.IV's employed in this battalion. There were instances when up to 75% of the vehicles available were unserviceable after long marches. The tactical number '645' is painted on the turret skirt in white and the Divisional emblem is also visible. The marking in front of the tactical number on the side is probably the Regimental standing bear emblem painted in red or black. Note the large hole in the rear edge of the side skirts, where an anti-tank round has exploded, preventing a potentially fatal hit on the tank. This is a Pz.Kpfw.IV Ausf.H.

An Sd.Kfz.251/1 Ausf.D traveling down a road through a village after the battle. The markings on the front of the vehicle have been overpainted with a light color by the crew as they tended to compromise the camouflage of the vehicle and provided an aiming point for enemy gunners.

Another Sd.Kfz.251/1 Ausf.D of the same unit photographed sometime later. This vehicle retains the Divisional emblem on the front plate and is covered with more camouflage material. The use of half-tracks by the Panzer-Grenadier Regiments gave the Germans tactical superiority over the motorized Soviet infantry despite the overwhelming numerical superiority of the Soviet divisions at a scale of about 3 to 1.

The Panzer-Grenadier Regiments had their own artillery support provided by a six gun battery of 15cm sIG33 Ausf.H or Ausf.M 'Grille' self-propelled guns built on the Pz.Kpfw.38(t) tank chassis. Most of the guns used by Pz.Gren.Rgt.12 and 33 were of the Ausf.H type.

The front of a heavily camouflaged 15cm sIG33 Ausf.M.

This Pz.Kpfw.V 'Panther' Ausf.G of I./Pz.Rgt.35 has been camouflaged with cut foliage and some bundles of straw picked up from the field. Two of the vehicle's side skirt plates are missing, a frequent occurrence when traveling through forested areas. Other than the conspicuous national cross on the front of the hull, no other markings are visible. During the whole month of August, 1944, 4.Panzer-Division claimed to have destroyed 240 tanks, 7 SPG's and 204 enemy guns.

Two photos of a Pz.Kpfw.V 'Panther' Ausf.G with a birch log hanging from the side as it advances through a harvested grain field. Part of the tactical number is visible showing the tank is from 1.Kompanie. The gun barrel is a very dark color probably indicating it is a replacement barrel which has not been painted.

The details of the cupola can be seen clearly in this photo of a 'Panther' commander as he views the terrain ahead through his field glasses. The significance of the rectangle painted below the episcope is unknown.

A Pz.Bef.Wg.V 'Panther' Ausf.G from I./Pz.Rgt.35 passing a camouflaged Sd.Kfz.7 half-tracked prime mover. The tank is finished with a three color camouflage scheme of green and brown over the dark sand base and also carries additional camouflage in the form of cut foliage, some of which has obscured part of the tactical number on the turret. An 'I' is partially visible though, identifying it as a staff vehicle of I.Abt.

The crew of this Pz.Kpfw.V 'Panther' Ausf.G has hung additional track links on the side of the turret in a way not commonly seen on the 'Panther'. A white tactical number '113' has been painted on the tracks indicating that their purpose is probably to provide additional armor protection. The camouflage scheme appears to be green lines and spots applied over the dark sand base on the hull and turret except for the gun barrel, which looks to be darker. This vehicle is probably a replacement for the 'Panther' Ausf.A seen earlier with the same tactical number.

Another photo of the same Panther, this time showing the whole vehicle. The spare tracklinks on the turret are obviously the ones normally mounted on the rear side of the hull.

An Sd.Kfz.251/1 Ausf.D traveling down a city street in Kurland, probably in September 1944. The location may be Doblen where 4.Panzer-Division was involved in heavy fighting in late September, after a three week period of limited activity.

61

A group of 'Panther' Ausf.G as seen from the turret of another 'Panther'. All of the vehicles have been camouflaged with spruce boughs in addition to their standard camouflage paint schemes. Note the open driver's hatch on the 'Panther' on the left shows the camouflage pattern has been painted on the top of the hull. The dark spot on the roof of the turret in the foreground is the shadow of the vehicle commander.

A closer view of the two 'Panthers' at the right of the above photo. Both are Ausf.G models and, judging by the lack of battle damage, appear to be relatively new. Note the difference in color of the gun barrels of these two tanks.

Two platoons of 'Panthers' of I./Pz.Rgt.35 converge on a road outside a village. All are finished in the standard camouflage pattern of this period, green and brown spots over the dark sand base and with plenty of spruce boughs added to supplement the camouflage.

A 'Panther' Ausf.G with the tactical number '111' crossing a grain field. During the battles around Doblen, the tank crews of I./Pz.Rgt.35 claimed to have destroyed 9 tanks, 1 SPG and many guns without a loss to themselves.

A 'Panther' Ausf.A kicks up a cloud of dust as it catches up with the rest of the platoon. The object in the foreground is the gun cleaning rod tube mounted on the rear of the engine deck of another 'Panther'. The antenna that is visible just behind is actually mounted on an Sd.Kfz.250/3 parked next to it.

Another view of the Sd.Kfz.250/3 showing it to be a 'Neu' version which also has been completely covered in spruce boughs for additional camouflage. The spare track links on the 'Panther' are visible in the foreground. During September, 4.Panzer-Division fought defensive battles in the Doblen area and, later on, in October near Venta. Major Schultze of I./Pz.Rgt.35 led a successful counterattack in the area on October 9, when three Kampfgruppen of reinforced 4.Panzer-Division caught a Soviet unit in a crossfire. In the final stage of the battle, Kampfgruppe Hoffmann and Kampfgruppe Schultze broke the resistance of a Soviet infantry regiment, killing up to 200 men and taking 300 prisoners, including the Soviet commander. They also claimed 31 destroyed or captured guns. II./Pz.Gren.Rgt.12 played an important role in the fighting, supported by Pz.Kpfw.IV tanks of 7.Kompanie/Pz.Rgt.35, commanded by Oblt. Petrelli.

A 'Panther' Ausf.G from 2nd platoon of the 1st company with a three color camouflage scheme of large splotches of brown and green over the dark sand base. This pattern has made the tank appear very dark. On October 10, 4.Panzer-Division repulsed several Soviet attacks between the villages of Pikeliai and Leskawa.

A platoon of heavily camouflaged 'Panther' Ausf.G advancing on enemy positions in the early evening twilight. In the middle of October, 4.Panzer-Division was moved to the right wing of the German defense in Kurland, close to Libau, a harbor on the Baltic coast. On October 17, 1944, I./Pz.Rgt.35 had 21 serviceable Pz.Kpfw.V while II./Pz.Rgt.35 had only 5 Pz.Kpfw.IV and Pz.Jg.Abt.49 only 2 Jagdpanzer IV.

A column of Pz.Kpfw.V 'Panther' Ausf.A along with an Sd.Kfz.251/6 Ausf.B and an Sd.Kfz.251/1 Ausf.D, pause for a rest on the retreat from the Kurland Peninsula. Also visible in the photo are two motorcycle combinations, the front one of which is a BMW R75. The Divisional emblem can be seen painted on the front of its sidecar.

4.Panzer-Division staff officers salute an unidentified General visiting the front in his Steyr 1500A staff car. It has an interesting camouflage scheme of green, wavy lines over the dark sand base, partly obscured by both old and new mud.

The wet, autumn weather in Kurland produced the same results as it did in the Soviet Union. Even powerful vehicles such as this Sd.Kfz.7 half-tracked prime mover, seen towing a truck, had trouble negotiating a path through the muddy fields. Conditions such as this greatly hindered offensive operations.

An Opel Blitz S-type 3 ton truck completely bogged down in a muddy field. Note the Panzerfaust 60 carried on the brackets that normally would have held the pickaxe. A small white swastika emblem can be seen through the heavy mud coating the right mudguard, a most unusual marking for this type of vehicle. The truck is painted overall dark sand.

A coffin is loaded into the rear of an Sd.Kfz.251/6 Ausf.B. The bodies of soldiers killed in action were usually buried on the spot and moved to a cemetery afterwards when the front had moved. Almost none were buried in coffins, which would indicate that this is probably the body of a high ranking officer.

Three views of a new Schwerer Panzerspähwagen (2cm) (Sd.Kfz.234/1), which replaced the Pz.Kpfw.II Ausf.L 'Luchs' as the main combat vehicle of Pz.Aufkl.Abt.4. This photo is taken in January 1945 in the area of Danzig (Gdansk). The vehicle has been painted with a hard edge camouflage scheme of green and brown irregular patches over the dark sand base, applied using a brush. There are no visible markings other than the vehicle license number, WH-1868316, painted on the front and rear plate and a small national cross painted on the side of the turret.

A Pz.Kpfw.II Ausf.L 'Luchs' of the early production series first sent to Pz.Aufkl.Abt.4 in the fall of 1943. It is still finished in its summer camouflage paint scheme and retains a full set of spare idler wheel segments across the front of the hull. Despite its weaknesses, the 'Luchs' played an important role in all the battles of 4.Panzer-Division in more than four months of fighting in Kurland in 1944. They were often employed as standard tanks which supported small units of infantry during attacks. The toll on men and machines was great however, only 119 men remained fit for duty on October 30, 1944.

4.Panzer-Division commander's personal half-track, the well known Sd.Kfz.251/6 Ausf.B, parked next to two 'Luchs' of Pz.Aufkl.Abt.4 at the edge of a forest during the winter of 1944-45. It has been covered with a white winter camouflage paint coat and still displays the Divisional command pennant on the left mudguard and the horseshoe for good luck on the front plate. It must have had some effect as the Division staff utilized this vehicle throughout its service on the Eastern Front, covering several thousand kilometers in its travels.

A closeup of General Betzel's Sd.Kfz.251/6 Ausf.B half-track with General Betzel and Oberstleutnant von Gaudecker. The wooden box on the side of the hull is a field workshop addition and probably held tools or other vehicle equipment. Between January 5 and January 7, 1945, 4.Panzer-Division fought in the Dzukste area claiming 31 tanks, 87 guns, 6 SPG's and 5 other vehicles destroyed. They killed about 200 Russian soldiers and captured 41 more. Their own losses were 3 tanks destroyed on January 6.

Oberstleutnant von Gaudecker, commander of Pz.Gren.Rgt.33, reviews a situation map with General Betzel in his command half-track. The final actions of 4.Panzer-Division in Kurland took place in early January 1945. On January 8, the Division was withdrawn from the frontlines and on January 19, started to make their way from Libau to Danzig. The strength of the Division was very weak at this time. The Grenadier Regiments and Aufklärung Abteilung had an average of only 163 men each. It left behind 73 tanks, 12 self-propelled guns and over 300 other vehicles, most of which were in need of repair.

During the course of the war on the Eastern Front, no less than 66 men of 4.Panzer-Division were awarded the Ritterkreuz (Knight's Cross) for extraordinary valor against the Soviet Army. As well, there were 10 officers and NCO's who were awarded the Eichenlaub (Oakleaves) and one, Gen.Lt. von Saucken, who was awarded the Schwerten (Swords) on January 31, 1944.

Another 6 men were decorated with the award before June 22, 1941, including the Divisional commander during the invasion of Poland, Gen.Maj. Georg-Hans Reinhardt. The remainder were awarded after the fall of France.

Altogether, 83 men of the Division received this award.

26 year old Oberfeldwebel Eduard Ender of I./Pz.Jg.Abt.49 is congratulated by a member of his crew after he was awarded with the Knight's Cross on February 29, 1944. In one photo, he is shown in front of his Marder II self-propelled anti-tank gun with two of his crew. He has also previously been awarded the Iron Cross First Class, General Assault Badge (Grade I) and a gilt Wound Badge.

The commander of I./Pz.Gren.Rgt.33, Hptm. Joachim Diesener with his Sd.Kfz.251/3 Ausf.D command half-track. He was awarded the Knight's Cross on June 9, 1944. Among his other awards are the Iron Cross First Class, German Cross in Gold and a silver Close Combat Clasp. The vehicle has a new tactical number painted on the side, '4401', in black with a white outline. The top of the national cross is visible just below.

Within a few days of the successful battle for Kovel, two officers of Pz.Rgt.35 were awarded the Knight's Cross. Lt. Karl-Heinrich Gsell of 2.Kompanie was decorated on February 23, 1945 and Lt. Reinhard Peters of 4.Kompanie was decorated on February 29, 1945. Both men have also previously been awarded the Iron Cross First Class. One has the ribbon from the East Front Medal through the buttonhole in his lapel while the other has the ribbon bar for the East Front Medal and the bronze Tank Battle Badge pinned to his tunic.

69

Three photos of the ceremony where Obergefreiter Lambert Loibl, of I./Pz.Gren.Rgt.33 was awarded the Knight's Cross on June 9, 1944. Obergefreiter Loibl was one of the most decorated soldiers of 4.Panzer-Division, having already been awarded the Iron Cross First and Second Class, a silver Close Combat Clasp, silver Wound Badge and a bronze Tank Battle Badge. The slip-on attached onto his shoulder strap indicates that he is an officer aspirant. In the background of one photo, an Sd.Kfz.251/1 Ausf.D half-track of the Regiment can be seen as well as an MG42 set up on its tripod mount.

An unidentified officer, probably from I./Pz.Gren.Rgt.33, is awarded his Knight's Cross during another ceremony. He is wearing the Iron Cross First Class, a Close Combat Clasp, the German Cross in Gold and, possibly, a Tank Battle Badge. Of interest are the two 15cm sIG33 Ausf.H 'Grille' self-propelled howitzers in the background. The vehicles are in very good condition and have well painted camouflage schemes of brown and green over the dark sand base, including the roadwheels. The last two digits of the tactical number and a national cross are visible in one of the photos.

Oberstleutnant Gerlach von Gaudecker, the commander of Pz.Gren.Rgt.33, won his Knight's Cross on August 8, 1944, after a successful engagement against the Soviet Army near Warsaw earlier that month. He was born in Zuch, near Neustettin, on March 24, 1908 and was one of the most experienced officers in 4.Panzer-Division. Here, he is wearing the special reed green drill Panzer tunic introduced in mid-1942.

Another photo of Obst.Lt. von Gaudecker in his Sd.Kfz.251/3 Ausf.D half-track, studying maps with one of his staff officers and Hptm. Joachim Diesener. Note the thickness of the armored shield for the MG42.

Obst.Lt. von Gaudecker and Hptm. Diesener riding in an Sd.Kfz.251/6 Ausf.B command half-track.

Major Lothar Beukemann, the commander of Pz.Pi.Btl.79, photographed just after receiving his Knight's Cross on January 25, 1945. His other awards include the German Cross in Gold and the Iron Cross First Class.